DATE DUE

MAY 05 1992	
	NOV 21 1991
DEC 07 1994	
DEC 12 1998	

I.S.A.M. Monographs: Number 28

Afro-American Music, South Africa, and Apartheid

CHARLES HAMM

I.S.A.M. Monographs: Number 28

Afro-American Music, South Africa, and Apartheid

CHARLES HAMM

Institute for Studies in American Music
Conservatory of Music
Brooklyn College
of the City University of New York

Published by the Institute for Studies in American Music
Conservatory of Music
Brooklyn College of the City University of New York
Brooklyn, New York 11210

CONTENTS

I

Paul Simon's *Graceland*, a record album released in the late summer of 1986,[1] is shot through with the rhythms and instrumental sounds of South Africa's black contemporary popular music. Simon recorded many of the preliminary tracks in Johannesburg in the summer of 1985, with local musicians, then arranged for some of them to come to the United States for the final stages of recording and mixing, and to join him in live and televised promotional performances. Even though the sound of South African jive, or *mbaqanga*, was exotic for most Americans, the album quickly sold a million copies, then two million; several individual songs received a great deal of air play and placed high on *Billboard*'s "Hot 100" singles charts during the fall and winter of 1986–87; and Simon's "Graceland Tour," co-featuring some of the performers on the album as well as several expatriate South African musicians, became his most successful live appearance since his split with Art Garfunkel.

Graceland was produced at a time when the attention of the United States was very much focused on South Africa. While Simon was recording in that country, American television viewers were treated to almost nightly sequences of protests and demonstrations against the racial policies of the white minority government, brutal police and army retaliation, and intensely passionate and militant funerals for the victims. From a distance, it appeared that the country was moving toward all-out racial warfare. Demonstrations outside the South African Embassy in Washington led to daily arrests, often of public figures; students around the country attempted to persuade their schools to divest from companies doing business in South Africa; debates over the official American policy of "constructive engagement" with the South African government occupied the press and the Congress. Shortly after Simon's return to America, South Africa took even harsher steps to contain spreading unrest: a state of emergency was imposed on the most troubled areas, empowering security forces to detain known or suspected political activists without charge; the press was prohibited from witnessing or reporting most aspects of the continuing turmoil; when accounts of the beating and torture of detainees became too persistent to be ignored or doubted, the government simply took steps to shield members of the security forces from prosecution for such acts. At least several thousand blacks were killed by security forces, and tens of thousands of people of all races were held in detention. By the time *Graceland* was released, the South African government had extended the state of emergency to the entire country, the U. S. Congress was in the process of imposing economic and political sanctions, more and more educational and civil institutions were selling their stock in countries doing business in South Africa, and many American companies were closing their operations there.

Graceland was released against this backdrop, and surely the intense interest of so many Americans in anything having to do with South Africa helped its sales. The album itself created controversy. Simon was accused of violating a UNESCO boycott on performance in South Africa; the texts of his songs took no note of the struggle within the country, and Simon adamantly maintained a politically neutral stance; the South African government was delighted with Simon's "constructive engagement" with the local recording industry and apolitical elements of the black population, and songs from *Graceland* were played constantly on the state-controlled South African Broadcasting Corporation (SABC).

Simon's political insensitivity aside,[2] *Graceland* represents a historic closing of a circle. For more than a century American popular music, especially those genres derived from Afro-American styles, was imported into South Africa, influencing the music of that country. Paul Simon's successful incorporation of black South African musical styles into his own music represents one of the first important reversals of this flow.

In what follows I will address the questions of why American popular music has been so enthusiastically received in black South Africa, what cultural and political factors are involved in this history, and why the pendulum is beginning to swing in the other direction at just this moment.

*   *   *

For reasons to be laid out below, it seems best to deal with Afro-American/black South African relations in two stages, the first extending from the middle of the nineteenth century to 1948, the second from 1948 to the present.

Minstrel songs and dances were the first music connected in any way with the American black to reach South Africa. Dale Cockrell has found evidence of a local minstrel troupe in Durban as early as 1858, and the American Christy Minstrels visited the city in 1865.[3] David Coplan, in his seminal study of the popular music of black South Africa, has summarized what is known about minstrelsy in that country in the middle decades of the last century:

> The publication of a number of minstrel songs, including Thomas Rice's classic, 'Jim Crow,' by the Cape Town weekly *Die Versammelar* helped to popularise them in the Colony. In 1848, a troupe called Joe Brown's Band of Brothers became . . . 'the first band of vocalists who gave South Africa a taste for nigger part singing'. In the same

year, white South Africans who had recently seen performances in London of the 'refined' American company, the Ethiopian Serenaders, began a local company of the same name. In 1862, the white performers of the Harvey-Christy Minstrels, who combined lively dancing and earthy humour with concert pieces and sentimental ballads, toured South Africa to such acclaim that minstrelsy became a permanent part of the country's entertainment for the rest of the century.[4]

Veit Erlmann has amplified the latter statement:

> In the next three decades [after 1862], blackface minstrel shows became the dominant form of popular white musical and theatrical entertainment in South Africa, perhaps only second in popularity to the public lecture and the circus. Amateur minstrel troupes mushroomed in the most remote provincial towns, and in the major centers of English culture like Kimberley, Durban, and Cape Town audiences were often able to choose between two minstrel entertainments on the same night. British regiments soon had their own permanent minstrel troupes that enjoyed high patronage from the colonial ruling elite.[5]

This repertory was at best one step removed from the music of black Americans (white Americans composing and performing pieces supposedly reflective of black music and culture) and at worst four steps away (white South Africans imitating white Britons imitating the white American perception of blacks). One would not expect to learn anything about Afro-American music from studying white minstrelsy in South Africa, of course; but one can begin to see the image of black America projected through the medium of the minstrel show to white South Africans, and also to blacks, who were sometimes allowed to sit or stand in segregated areas during performances of minstrel shows for white audiences.

In the last decade of the century, South Africans had the opportunity to see and hear black American performers for the first time. Orpheus M. McAdoo, born of slave parents in Greensboro, North Carolina, landed in Cape Town in June 1890 with his Virginia Jubilee Singers and performed in various parts of the country for the next two years, for both white and black audiences, before sailing to Australia. The company returned to South Africa in 1895 for a further three years, though their performances were interrupted for some months in 1897 when McAdoo traveled to New York to recruit additional cast members.[6]

Even before the arrival of McAdoo's company, black South Africans had begun to imitate American minstrel music with as much enthusiasm as whites. Little specific information has been retrieved, since such matters were of no interest to the white population and therefore did not find their way into the press, though the *Natal Mercury* of 28 December 1880 did mention performance by the Kafir Christy

Minstrels, a "troupe of eight genuine natives, bones and all, who really get through their songs very well."[7] The prolonged presence of McAdoo's troupe in the country spurred even more minstrel activity among blacks. Will P. Thompson left the Virginia Jubilee Singers to form groups of his own with African performers, including the Diamond Minstrels (in Kimberley) and the Balmoral Amateur Minstrels.[8] The "coloured" population of Cape Town organized social clubs which paraded and competed against one another during Carnival season, dressed in costumes imitative of traditional minstrel garb, carrying American flags, singing pieces—to the accompaniment of banjos, among other instruments—based on various types of minstrel songs.[9] Minstrel songs were performed at school and community concerts; in the early twentieth century a few members of the black elite were able to purchase phonographs and thus hear recordings of minstrel music, mostly by English performers. By the first and second decades of the present century there were many black minstrel companies, often formed while their members were together in mission schools, performing in black townships throughout South Africa; among those active in Natal were the Brave Natalian Coons, the Western Minstrels (based at Adams Mission), the Highland Coons, and the Inanda Native Singers.[10] When commercial recordings by black performers began to be made in the 1920s and '30s, first by musicians taken to London and then in Johannesburg, minstrel companies supplied a substantial amount of the repertory.

The penetration of American minstrel music into black South Africa can be seen as progressing in three stages:

(i) **Importation**. The music was brought into the country by foreign performers, or by local white entertainers who had heard it while abroad; later, phonograph discs were imported from abroad.

(ii) **Imitation**. Black South African musicians performed minstrel songs in the style in which they were done in the United States or Britain. Sometimes pieces from the American repertory were performed in English, as when James Bland's "Oh! Dem Golden Slippers" was sung on a program in Kimberley in 1892[11] or when the Inanda Native Singers performed Stephen Foster's "Old Folks at Home" and C. A. White's "I'se Gwine Back to Dixie."[12] Sometimes American tunes were sung to African texts, or new melodies were fashioned in close imitation of American models. "Imali Yami," recorded by John Mavimbela and Company in the 1930s [Gallo Singer Bantu Records, GE 34], with a solo male voice singing to the accompaniment of a humming chorus, banjo, and harmonica, has a tune indistinguishable from nineteenth-century American popular stage melodies in melodic contour and phraseology.

(iii) **Assimilation**. Stylistic features of American minstrel songs were absorbed into black South African performance traditions. Thus acculturation had taken place, a repertory had been created drawing on both indigenous and foreign elements, and new genres appeared distinct from those found elsewhere. In order to deal with this third stage, it is necessary to have some understanding of the traditional, pre-colonization music of South Africa.

Though the region now defined by the political boundaries of the Republic of South Africa is home to a complex network of different ethnic groups,[13] and the present white minority government has labelled and attempted to isolate a dozen or so of these for its own political purposes, all blacks in the area speak some type of Bantu language,[14] and in fact contemporary scholarship suggests a division into only two large language groups: the Nguni, subdivided into Zulu, Xhosa, and Swazi; and the Sotho, with a much larger number of sub-groups, some—such as the Venda and Tsonga—related to ethnic groups in the neighboring countries of Zimbabwe and Mozambique.[15] There is considerable traditional cultural consistency among all these peoples, who belong to pastoral and agricultural societies, with cattle at the core of their political, economic, and social structures.

Traditional music of this part of the continent differs in some ways from that of the rest of sub-Sahara Africa. The dominant performance medium is the unaccompanied chorus, usually with one or more solo voices pitted against a larger group in call-and-response patterns. This music functions in a ritual or ceremonial context, as part of communal celebration of individual rites of passage or of important points along the seasonal and agricultural cycles. But it makes little sense to impose a Western distinction between ceremonial and recreational function on these celebrations, during which dancing, singing, and beer-drinking serve as much to bring pleasure to the participants as to ritualize the occasion. At weddings, for instance, members of the two families may engage in dancing and singing competitions, in a way that strikes the Western observer as more entertainment than ritual.[16]

There is also solo song, accompanied by an ostinato-playing instrument such as the musical bow, or in the northeast some form of the *mbira*; this genre often functions to preserve the history and lineage of a clan or other social group, or as purely personal expression. There is no tradition of melodic instrumental music, with the exception of flute music played by herd boys; reed-pipe ensembles, found in some areas, assign notes of the "melody" to different instruments, as in European bell ringing. Amazingly, for Africa, there is no tradition of drumming. Choral music may be accompanied by hand clapping, foot stomping, or the rattling of shells attached to the legs of the performers, but drums came to this region only with European military and dance music.

The two most important stylistic features of traditional music in South Africa might be taken as metaphors of general cultural patterns. First, both vocal and instrumental pieces unfold over brief, constantly reiterated structures: in choral music these take the form of recurring vertical combinations of notes, or "chords"; in instrumental music, and instrumental accompaniment to vocal music, one hears an insistently repeated melodic-rhythmic ostinato. Life in sub-Sahara Africa is perceived as progressing cyclically—through seasons, agricultural phases, the human rites of passage. Music also moves cyclically, always turning back on itself at the most basic structural level, unlike Western music, which marches inexorably along a linear, goal-oriented path in its progress toward an inevitable denouement.

Secondly, traditional music is built horizontally of different layers of sound, each contributing to the whole while maintaining some degree of individuality. As Andrew Tracey has put it, "the independence of the various parts in a piece of [African] music, unified by the recurring cycle, can be taken as [a] metaphor for the traditional individuality of personality and behaviour allowed and even expected within the bounds of the tightly-structured social patterns of African life."[17]

The assimilation or "Africanization" of minstrel music involved the absorption of stylistic elements from the American repertory into pieces retaining the two general stylistic elements just described. Early commercial phonograph discs allow us to hear this process taking place. "Into Yami," as performed by the Willie Gumede Banjo Band [Gallotone Singer GE 948], sounds superficially like an American minstrel piece, with one banjo "picking" the tune accompanied by several strummed banjos and a bones player. Listening a bit more closely, however, one can hear that the entire piece is built over reiteration of the harmonic pattern I–IV–V–V; that the "melody" could more accurately be described as repeated and varied melodic patterning; and that the three contrapuntal threads (melody, strummed accompaniment, rhythm) persistently maintain their own individuality, with no thematic reference to the other parts. A more complex example is "Ingqaqa—Mazinyo We' Mkwenyana," recorded by Kuzwayo's Zulu Dance Band [HMV JP 19]. Two lead instruments, concertina and banjo, play clearly differentiated melodic patterns, sometimes consecutively and sometimes simultaneously; a guitar gives out a constantly repeated line which functions both as a bass part and a rhythmic accompaniment; and a drummer, playing a rudimentary trap set, completes the ensemble—all this taking place over an unchanging four-bar harmonic foundation. The piece is African, though the ancestry of some of its elements in American minstrel music is apparent enough.

Traces of the impact of minstrelsy on black South African styles persist to the present, for instance in music performed by small vocal groups of workers living in single-sex hostels, in Natal.[18] Ladysmith Black Mambazo, a contemporary *ingom 'ebusuku* group of eight to ten male singers which performed in the United Staes in 1986–87 following the release of Paul Simon's *Graceland,* gave American audiences a chance to see how much the stage movement of present-day groups can invoke the minstrel tradition.

The same scholarly techniques used to reconstruct the history of minstrel music in South Africa enable us to trace the same three stages of penetration of the other types of Afro-American music brought to South Africa before 1948: gospel songs, ragtime, spirituals, early syncopated dance music, early jazz, and swing. For each, documentary evidence tells us when it was imported, and under what circumstances; early recordings preserve examples of the stages of imitation and assimilation; contemporary performance practice informs us of the later stages of assimilation and the extent to which these styles persist to the present.

American vocal styles have a particularly rich history of penetration into black South Africa, which is hardly surprising in a culture so grounded in choral music itself. Cockrell has shown that an edition of Moody and Sankey's *Gospel Hymns* with texts translated into Zulu was published in Durban in 1876, that spirituals were sung in that city as early as 1889 (by a forty-voice white choir), and that McAdoo's Virginia Jubilee Singers included spirituals on their programs in 1890. He observes that gospel hymns "remain a staple of church congregations and choirs, school choirs, male quartet[s] . . . and such popular black South African recording groups as the King's Messengers Quartet" and that "by the early years of this century, [the spiritual] had become a staple of the repertory of black choirs, both professional and amateur."[19] Erlmann has added more details: the title of the collection published by 1876 was *Hymns in Kafir, From Sacred Songs and Solos, By J. D. Sankey*; by the early 1900s American gospel hymns were being printed in the tonic sol-fa notation used in black musical education; by 1908 the British Zonophone Company issued eight discs of Sankey and Moody hymns sung by a group of Swazi chiefs visiting England.[20] And after the first stages of penetration and imitation, indigenous choral genres combining traditional styles with American elements proliferated in the twentieth century.

Taking as another example a more recent genre, vocal swing, one sees the same processes at work. Advertisements and reviews in newspapers, information from record companies, inventories of personal and institutional collections of phonograph discs, and reminiscences by persons now in their fifties and sixties all inform us that recordings by black American vocal groups, usually trios or quartets accompanied by a rhythm section, were *imported* and widely sold in South Africa from the late 1930s into the '50s. One can even identify the Mills Brothers and the Ink Spots as the most popular of these. Documentary and recorded evidence tells us that black groups in Johannesburg and elsewhere began *imitating* this style soon after it was imported. One of the first, and surely the most successful, was the Manhattan Brothers, formed in the mid-1930s while the four of them—Ronnie Sehume, Joseph Kulwane Mogotsi, Rufus Koza, Dambuza Mdledle—were classmates at the Pimville Government School.[21] They came to widespread public attention in the 1940s through live performances on the South African Broadcasting Corporation and at the Bantu Men's Social Club in Johannesburg, and with their numerous recordings for Gallo, the largest South African recording company. Many of their early recordings are "cover" versions, sung in one of the African languages, of pieces written by white Tin Pan Alley songwriters and recorded by black American groups: "Yes-Suh" by Andy Razaf and Saxie Dowell [Gallotone Singer Bantu Records GE 937]; "U Mama" ("Mamma, I Wanna Make Rhythm") by Richard Byron, M. K. Jerome, and Walter Kent [Gallotone GE 938]. But *assimilation* was taking place almost from the beginning. "Umlilo" [Gallotone GE 939] is apparently as derivative of vocal swing in general style as the other early repertory of the Manhattan Brothers, but unlike the American pieces just mentioned, which all share the uniquitous AABA pattern of late Tin Pan Alley song, this piece progresses in eight-beat phrases built over a single insistent harmonic underpinning. A somewhat later piece by the Manhattan Brothers, "Unonkisa Kae" [Gallotone GB 1819; rel. 1953], has moved even further towards "Africanization": it unfolds over a four-bar harmonic ostinato (I–IV–V–I), and there are hints of call-and-response patterns among the voices.

Vocal swing proliferated in the 1950s, and a mere listing of the names of some commercially recorded groups not only gives a sense of the popularity of this genre but underlines the indebtedness to American models: the African Inkspots, the Boogie Five, the Boogie Brothers, the African Brothers, the Gandy Brothers, the Bogard Brothers, the Crown Brothers, the Harari Swing Brothers, the King Cole Basies, the King Cole Boogies, the King Cole Porters, the Black Broadway Boys. Nor has this genre disappeared altogether today. The Beam Brothers, whose music is still available on such LPs as *Thuli Wami* [Gallo: Motella BL 58], perform in essentially the style of the 1950s, and the Soul Brothers and other popular vocal jive or *mbaqanga* groups draw on elements of vocal swing, though their rhythmic and instrumental vocabulary is more contemporary.

With time and patience, more details of the importation, imitation, and assimilation of American music before 1948 will be teased out of the materials available to scholars. This was not a process taking place in a void, however, but part of a larger complex of relations between South Africa and the United States. It is this more general picture that must be studied if one is to understand why so much American music was brought into South Africa, and what role this music played at various stages of the black African struggle for cultural and political autonomy.

*   *   *

Historically, American relations with South Africa have been significantly different from those with other parts of the continent. No slaves were brought directly to the New World from the geographical area now encompassed by the Republic of South Africa. First contact came with the docking of American ships at Cape Town in the eighteenth century, to establish economic and political relations with the Dutch who had settled there, and later with the British who took control; but these first American visitors had virtually no contact with the indigenous population.

The first direct American involvement with black South Africans came in the 1830s, through the church. The American Board of Commissioners for Foreign Missions, based in London, sent six missionaries to the Zulu kingdom in the 1830s, and other American missionaries found their way to the Transvaal in the same decade.[22] The American Daniel Lindley served as pastor to both Zulus and Afrikaner Voortrekkers in the 1840s, and in 1853 the American Board established a first mission school in Zululand, Adams College, which was soon followed by another at Inanda. This was consonant with Governor Sir George Gray's policy in the Cape Colony of "civilization by mingling," an attempt to lessen friction between white and black by allowing religious groups to establish schools for blacks.[23] The process of Christianization at these missions and schools included, of course, the singing of hymns from the white Protestant nineteenth-century repertory.

Two important points must be stressed, before we go on. First, until the 1890s, American relations with black South Africans involved only white persons from the United States, most of them connected with the church. Second, these Americans were not cast in the role of colonizers and exploiters, as were the Dutch and British who had forcibly occupied the land and, with military and economic power, subjugated the indigenous population, depriving black people of land ownership and political autonomy. Though subsequent scholarship would assign Christianity an important role in the process of colonization, through pacification of dispossessed populations, no one at the time entertained such a notion, and white missionaries and educators were seen by blacks as doers of good deeds.

The members of Orpheus McAdoo's minstrel troupe were among the first black Americans to have direct contact with black South Africans. In 1893 several local white entrepreneurs organized an "African Native Choir" among students attending mission schools in Kimberley and Lovedale. After performing in the United Kingdom and Canada, the group came to the United States; again, music was the initiator of early relations between African and American blacks. Stranded in the Midwest when funds ran out and their white manager abandoned them, members of the group were enrolled at Wilberforce and Lincoln universities, with the aid of the black African Methodist Episcopal Church (AME). Some earned degrees, and several played important roles in the formation of a new urbanized black elite when they returned to South Africa.[24] At about the same time, two Xhosa Methodist ministers, Mangena Mokone and James Dwane, became disaffected with the policies of the English church in South Africa and announced a new affiliation with the American AME. In 1898 Bishop H. M. Turner of the AME came to South Africa to strengthen ties between the American and African branches of the church, personally ordaining sixty-five local ministers while in the country. The result of all this was the emergence of the South African AME as a "large, well-organized all-black church with transatlantic ties, . . . the church of the educated African townspeople, whose broadened horizons led them to a strong identification with the struggles of the American Negro."[25]

The AME established Wilberforce Institute at Evaton in the Transvaal, modeled on the American Tuskeegee Institite, in 1897. John L. Dube, one of the handful of black South Africans able to pursue higher education in America, educated at Tuskeegee and elsewhere in the United States in 1887–92 and 1897–99 and a disciple of Booker T. Washington, founded Ohlange Institute in Natal in 1901. Dube also began editing *Ilanga lase Natal*, an African-language journal, in 1903.

A network for interaction between the black populations of South Africa and the United States, which was to remain in place for several decades, was thus taking shape by the beginning of the twentieth century: a handful of black Americans, probably no more than 100 in the nineteenth century, many of them entertainers and clergymen, found their way to South Africa;[26] an even smaller number of black South Africans, mostly political and educational leaders of the tiny black elite, came to the United States. Solomon Plaatje, writer and politician and one of the founders of the African National Congress, was in America in 1920–22; Reuben Caluza, who played a central role in the creation of several genres of black South African music, studied with Nathaniel Dett at Hampton Institute early in the 1930s. But musical flow was one way, with Afro-American styles brought to Africa by occasional live performance and much more importantly by the mass media (printed music, phonograph discs, eventually films), while Americans remained ignorant of the music of South Africa.

In order to begin to understand the inordinate impact of Afro-American culture on black South Africa, out of all proportion to this amount of direct contact, one must consider the separate histories of the two black populations.

Until the end of the nineteenth century, there seemed to be little common ground between them. Africans were brought to the United States in large numbers only after the indigenous population, the American Indians, had been subdued and a plantation economy established. Black Americans were slaves in an alien country, with no ancestral ties to the land; their languages and social structures gradually disappeared, to be replaced by a new common language (English), a new religion (Christianity), and a new common identity (as African-Americans) pieced together over a period of time from a patchwork of pan-African cultural survivals and elements of the dominant American society in which they found themselves. They were a minority black population in a white land. Beginning in 1863 they were legally free to vote, own land, and hold public office, though these theoretical freedoms were mostly denied them by various strategies of the white population.

Most black South Africans continued to occupy their traditional lands after military subjugation, though the white population gradually took over the best land for its own use. They preserved their own languages and social structures, though the latter were gradually modified by contact with Europeans. Although a majority population, far outnumbering white colonizers, they were unable to utilize their numerical superiority for effective resistance because of superior European military and economic force, and because there was no tradition of black unity in the region. Though slavery was abolished in South Africa much earlier than in the United States—on 1 December 1834—blacks had few legal rights in the British-controlled Natal and the Cape and virtually none in the two Afrikaner Republics, the Orange Free State and the Transvaal.

Despite these differences, by the beginning of the twentieth century the social and political condition of blacks in the two countries had come to a remarkable convergence, one of enforced racial segregation:

> Between the 1890s and the 1960s, the notorious Jim Crow laws of the southern states regulated inter-racial contacts in public places or facilities in such a way as to exclude blacks from most accommodations available to whites. The separate amenities or institutions provided for blacks were—despite the legal fiction of "separate but equal"—glaringly inferior and emblematic of a degraded social status. This pattern of mandatory social segregation was paralleled in the political sphere by the exclusion of most blacks from the electorate through a variety of voting restrictions put into effect by state legislation or constitutional provision between the 1880s and 1910....

In South Africa, the emergence of segregationalism as a deliberate public policy coincided quite closely with the establishment of a self-governing union [in the first decade of the 20th century]. . . . The principal motive for prescribing separate living areas, public facilities, and political institutions was to restrict the power and privileges of the African majority to such an extent that the preservation of white minority rule would be absolutely assured. But a more idealistic rationale was often provided for the benefit of those who doubted the justice of these policies. It was argued that Europeans and "natives" differed so greatly in cultural backgrounds and levels of civilization that it was best to allow each group to "develop along its own lines."[27]

However, both groups perceived that of the two, American blacks had attained a much more favorable position. Orpheus McAdoo, writing back to the States after his first experiences in South Africa, observed:

There is no country in the world where prejudice is so strong as here in [South] Africa. The native today is treated as badly as ever the slave was treated in Georgia. Here in Africa the native laws are most unjust; such as any Christian people would be ashamed of. Do you credit a law in a civilized county compelling every man of dark skin, even though he is a citizen of another country, to be in his house by 9 o'clock at night, or he is arrested? . . . These laws exist in the Transvaal and Orange Free State, which are governed by the Dutch, who place every living creature before the native.[28]

For their part, black Africans were impressed by the dress and the demeanor of McAdoo and members of his troupe, by seeing them "[move] about with all the ease and freedom among the white people that a high state of civilization and education alone can give,"[29] and by hearing them describe the achievements of their race in America:

Hear! Today they have their own schools, primary, secondary and high schools, and also universities. They are run by them without the help of the whites. They have magistrates, judges, lawyers, bishops, ministers and evangelists, and school masters. Some have learned a craft such as building etc. etc. When will the day come when the African people will be like the Americans? When will they stop being slaves and become nations with their own government?[30]

And the few black South Africans who had found their way to America brought back similar reports.

American blacks would have been amazed by such favorable portrayals of their condition. Most of them still lived under economic and political restraints scarcely different from those of slave days. Only a few had been able to take advantage of educational opportunities and form a small black elite. The South African perception was based on limited contact with a tiny and unrepresentative group of American blacks, chiefly educators, entertainers, and religious leaders; and it was further distorted by the medium of print, largely controlled by whites in both the United States and South Africa, which persisted in offering inaccurate and even deliberately false images of black life in America.

In the capitalist society that the United States had become by the end of the nineteenth century, music was increasingly produced as a commodity to be marketed for profit, with decisions of repertory and style largely in the hands of capital and entrepreneurs. What South Africans, from a distance, took to be authentic Afro-American music was in fact selected and mediated for commercial presentation to American whites, who purchased the great majority of the printed music and phonograph discs produced in the nineteenth and early twentieth centuries. For instance:

¶ The music style of the minstrel show was shaped by white entertainers performing for white audiences; melodic, harmonic, and formal patterns were drawn chiefly from the traditional Anglo-American repertory and the popular stage music of the 1820s and '30s, modified in the 1850s by Stephen Foster.[31] True enough, at least two of the instruments used in early minstel shows, the banjo and the bones, were Afro-American in origin, and the earliest banjo style (using non-harmonic ostinato patterns) appears to reflect African elements, but this type of playing had disappeared from the stage by the time the minstrel show came to South Africa. Blacks there had no opportunity to hear authentic American black dance music for banjo and fiddle, only white parodies of it.

¶ The gospel hymns of Sankey and Moody belong to a long tradition of religious music created by white composers for white congregations.[32] They have nothing to do with Afro-American music in melody and structure, though in time a distinctive black performance style grew up around such music. But black South Africans had no opportunity to hear black Americans sing gospel music.

¶ Though spirituals drew on texts and tunes created by black slaves, they reached South Africa in triadic, tonal, homorhythmic arrangements of the sort first popularized by the Fisk Jubilee Singers in the late 1860s, then emulated by choral groups at other black schools and by professional minstrel companies. These arrangements were made first by whites (George L. White at Fisk University, Thomas Fenner at Hampton Institute), later by blacks trained in European musical styles; they were intended chiefly for white audiences.[33] South Africans knew American spirituals only in this mediated form, not as they were sung in black churches with call-and-response patterns, percussive accompaniment, and other African survivals.

¶ Ragtime likewise reached South Africa in a form mediated for the consumption of white Americans, as piano pieces by white composers and "coon songs" by white Tin Pan Alley songwriters. Rural ragtime and the black dance music from which it drew its characteristic rhythms were unknown in South Africa.

¶ No black American performers of early syncopated dance music, early jazz, or swing found their way to South Africa; so blacks there knew this music only through the media (phonograph records, films, printed music) or from an occasional white performer, usually British, who himself had only second-hand knowledge of the style. Recordings of this music available to black South Africans had gone through two levels of mediation. In America, the "jazz" offered by major record companies was played by white musicians, or by blacks playing or singing in styles thought to be appropriate for white consumption; music by black musicians intended for black audiences was marketed by small companies, and on a regional basis only, on "race records." Since blacks made up only a small percentage of the market for phonograph records in South Africa until the 1950s, the selection and marketing of American "jazz" by local record companies was based largely on its potential appeal to whites in that country, and blacks could choose only from what was made available by this process. As a result, black South Africans were able to hear "jazz" songs by Irving Berlin and instrumental "jazz" by Paul Whiteman, but no early New Orleans, Chicago, or New York jazz. They could hear Al Jolson, Bing Crosby, Lena Horne, Nat King Cole, Ella Fitzgerald, Frank Sinatra, Billie Holiday, and Johnny Mathis, but the great blues singers— from Ma Rainey, Blind Lemon Jefferson, Bessie Smith, and Papa Charlie Jackson through Leroy Carr, Sleepy John Estes, Big Bill Broonzy, and Robert Johnson— remained unknown in Africa. As noted above, the Mills Brothers and the Ink Spots became widely popular in South Africa, but blacks there never even heard of Gary Davis, the Excelsior Quartet, the Blue Jay Singers, or other black gospel groups of the era.

David Coplan has offered a brilliant and comprehensive discussion of how black South African contact with Afro-Americans in the late nineteenth and early twentieth centuries helped "foster a racial self-respect that became a basis for non-violent struggle against a society determined to crush African aspirations."[34] Elsewhere, in discussing the ways in which the music of American blacks played an important role in establishing their own self-identity, in shaping resistance to white oppression, and in furthering cultural and political aspirations, he develops the thesis that, because of "similarities in the sociohistorical experience of black Americans and South Africans, including rapid urbanisation and industrialisation, and racial oppression, [and] similarities in the kinds of musical resources available to both peoples in their urban areas, and in basic African principles of composition and performance," Afro-American music served as a model for "black South African urban cultural adaptation, identity and resistance."[35]

Coplan's work is important and convincing enough to make it unnecessary for other writers to say more on this subject. But just as African perception of the status and achievements of black Americans was shaped and distorted by the limitation of direct contact to a handful of relatively privileged individuals from each group, and by dependence on the media for information, so the African perception of black American music was limited by similar factors. It seems fair to generalize that most "Afro-American" music imported into South Africa before the middle of the twentieth century was mediated by and acceptable to white Americans. It was imprinted with white taste and white styles; and in the process of being transformed into a commodity for white consumers, it had lost much of the African identity so unmistakable in many forms of Afro-American music performed and enjoyed by blacks themselves at this time.

Black South African admiration for black American political and cultural achievement, up to the middle of the present century, was based to some degree on highly selective and often distorted information and images. The fact that this situation began to change around mid-century accounts for the gradually shifting African attitudes towards black Americans, and for the division of the present paper into two parts.

II

For most of the first half of the twentieth century, similarities in the social and political conditions of blacks in South Africa and the United States outweighed the many differences.

The screws of racial segregation were tightening in the United States. One state after another enacted legislation making it difficult or impossible for blacks to vote, and legalizing the segregation of public and private facilities. The Supreme Court itself upheld the segregation of public accomodations, in the *Plessy v. Ferguson* decision of 1896. Backlash against the massive new waves of immigration from the southern Mediterranean and Central Europe, stressing the threat to the culture of "native Americans" from the "impure stock" pouring into the country by the millions in the decades surrounding the turn of the century, led to much stricter immigration policies[36] and also to increasing intolerance of other ethnic minorities, blacks above all. Racist literature proliferated, and the Ku Klux Klan, revitalized, spread to all parts of the country.

In South Africa the few civil rights accorded the black population were eroded, and a steady stream of new legislation intensified racial separation. The Native Lands Act of 1913 forced blacks to live only in "reserves," and other legislation severely inhibited their migration to urban areas. The Mine and Works Act of Union Parliament (1911) established racial segregation in industry; the Colour Bar Act (1926) excluded blacks from skilled jobs on the mine fields. Only a few blacks, in Cape Province, had the franchise, and the last of these were removed from voter rolls in 1936. Both custom and law inhibited social contact, beyond employer-employee relations, between black and white.

The first organized resistance to enforced segregation, in both countries, was spearheaded by the black elite. A conference held in New York City on 30 May 1909 "for the discussion of present evils, the voicing of protests, and the renewal of the struggle for civil and political liberty" was attended largely by black educators, professional people, and religious leaders. A second conference, in May 1910, resulted in the founding of the National Association for the Advancement of Colored People (NAACP), with the educator and author W. E. B. DuBois chosen as the first executive. In South Africa, a meeting in Bloemfontein on 8 January 1912 of "several hundred of South Africa's most prominent African citizens: professional men, chieftains, ministers, teachers, clerks, interpreters, landholders, businessmen, journalists, estate agents, building contractors and labour agents"[37] led to the formation of the South African Native National Congress, renamed the African National Congress (ANC) in 1923. The first president was John Dube, founder and headmaster of the Ohlange Institute in Natal, mentioned above as having studied in the United States; Solomon Plaatje, named secretary, was later to come to America also; and the treasurer, Pixley ka Izaka Seme, had studied law in London.

But underlying these surface similarities was an overriding, fundamental difference: racial segregation was contrary to the Constitution of the United States, as amended in the middle of the nineteenth century; but racial segregation was legally enshrined in South Africa. Events of the late 1940s and early '50s were to underline this difference and result in a dramatic divergence in the civil status of the two black populations.

Soon after the end of World War II, American blacks launched an aggressive drive to achieve the equality that should have been theirs as citizens of the United States but was in practice denied them by state and municipal legislation, and by social custom. The Supreme Court decision of 1954, in *Brown v. Board of Education of Topeka,* that racial segregation in the public schools was unconstitutional, rang the death knell for the doctrine of "separate but equal" facilities. In 1956 blacks in Montgomery, Alabama, staged a boycott to protest segregated seating on city buses; on 13 November the Supreme Court ruled that such segregation on public transportation was unconstitutional. The governor of Arkansas attempted to resist court-ordered racial segregaton of Little Rock High School in 1957; President Eisenhower sent members of the U.S. armed forces to enforce the court order, and nine black students entered the school. In these and other cases, the pattern was the same: if American blacks had the determination and courage to insist on their legal rights, the federal government had no choice but to support them.

But not so in South Africa. In 1948 the National Party, after campaigning on a platform of Afrikaner nationalism and resistance to "the erosion of white power," won control of Parliament. New legislation to further strengthen and codify racial separation was put into effect almost immediately: the Prohibition of Mixed Marriages Act (1949); the Population Registration Act (1950), requiring every South African to be classified and registered according to racial category; the Group Areas Act (1950), confining each population group to specified residential areas. In response, the ANC joined other organizations in staging the Defiance Campaign of 1952, in which thousands of blacks invaded segregated facilities, offering no resistance to arrest. A National Action Council for the Congress of the People, held near Johannesburg in 1955, adopted a "Freedom Charter" insisting that South Africa should be a non-racial society, with equal status and opportunity for all people. A three-month-long bus boycott in Alexandra township, in Johannesburg, protesting fare increases, was the most determined in a series dating back to 1940.

These strategies were similar to those pursued by American blacks, but the outcomes were strikingly different. Since national laws were being violated by the black invasion of segregated facilities, the force of the South African government was used to quell the Defiance Campaign. More than eight thousand persons were arrested,[38] many of the leaders were placed under banning orders restricting future political activity, and even more harsh racial legislation was passed. The Congress at which the Freedom Charter was adopted was "brought to an exciting close by the arrival of a large detachment of policemen bearing sten guns in the afternoon of the second day. They took over the speakers' platform, confiscated all the documents they could find, announced that they had reason to believe that treason was being contemplated, and took the names and addresses of all the delegates."[39] And the government refused to mediate in the bus boycotts, staged against a private mass transport company.

Thus the power and authority of the national government was used to maintain racial segregation and discrimination, not to lessen it as in the United States.

*   *   *

Rock 'n' roll, emerging in the United States as a dynamic and even revolutionary new form of popular music in the mid-1950s, played a quite different role in America and South Africa.

The first truly interracial American popular music,[40] rock 'n' roll drew elements of its style from black music, chiefly rhythm-and-blues, and also from the music of white Southerners. Its early stars were both black (Chuck Berry, Fats Domino, Little Richard) and white (Bill Haley, Elvis Presley, Jerry Lee Lewis, the Everly Brothers, Buddy Holly). The audience was likewise interracial: data in *Billboard* and other trade journals tells us that blacks and whites bought phonograph records by many of the same performers, and listened to the same music on the radio; and early live shows, such as those organized by Alan Freed or put on at military bases, played for racially mixed audiences. Whether one believes that popular music mirrors contemporary society, or agrees with Jacques Attali that music is prophetic,[41] early rock 'n' roll must be seen as a powerful statement that the United States was moving towards an interracial society in the 1950s—a view further supported by the fact that persons and institutions most resistant to racial integration were most strongly opposed to this music.[42]

Given the historic identification of black South Africans with Afro-American political struggles and music, one would have expected enthusiastic African reception of rock 'n' roll. But this is not what happened.

Rock 'n' roll arrived in South Africa in the same way it came to other European and post-Colonial countries. Phonograph records by the Crew Cuts, Bill Haley, and Elvis Presley were available soon after their release in America, and the distribution of Presley's films *Love Me Tender* and *Jailhouse Rock* in early 1957 gave such a boost to his popularity that a poll conducted by the *Sunday Times* of Johannesburg in 1959 identified him as the top male vocalist of all time—replacing Bing Crosby, incidentally—and "Jailhouse Rock" was found to be the most popular single disc in the history of the record industry in South Africa.[43]

As elsewhere, rock 'n' roll became a battleground for the generational confrontations of the 1950s. A journalist correctly linked this music to "those hordes of sloppy, be-jeaned louts and their girl friends who cause so much trouble in South Africa,"[44] and rock 'n' roll and its audiences were condemned from the pulpit and lecture podium and by the state-controlled SABC (South African Broadcasting Corporation), which refused to air rock music even into the 1960s on the grounds that "offering the young South African something more than mere beat music is in harmony with and linked to a constantly growing desire in young people nowadays for programmes of a more serious kind."[45] But South Africa was a capitalist country, and despite opposition to this music from the ruling National Party and the powerful Nederdruits Gere-formeerde Kerk (NGK), recording companies continued to realize unprecedented profits from marketing rock 'n' roll among the white youth of the country, who were sharing the fruits of a post-war economic boom.

Some benefits of this new prosperity were filtering down to the black population as well, and in an attempt to boost record sales even more, several companies adopted strategies for marketing this music among blacks: releasing selected rock 'n' roll records on 78-rpm discs (since most blacks owned battery-operated playback equipment running only at this speed); distributing these to retail outlets catering to black customers; and sending review copies to publications aimed at black readers. Todd Matshikiza reviewed three records distributed by Trutone Africa Ltd. in the July 1955 issue of the slick monthly *Drum*: "Boys, it's real 'jiving' when you get to Mercury Records. American singers and bands: Just dig these numbers [which included "Sh-Boom"]. The CREW CUTS—one of America's all-time high groups"; and in July 1956 he began a review of Bill Haley's "Rock Around the Clock" with "You've probably got interested in the new American craze the 'Rock' which pounds with rhythms even more exciting than the grooviest jive tempos."

Reviews and feature articles dealing with rock 'n' roll give evidence that this music penetrated black South African culture to some degree between 1956 and 1958. Casey Motsisi described a party in Western Native Township, near Johannesburg, in the May 1958 issue of *Drum*:

> This here midnite party is participating. There's enough booze to keep Mr Kruschev blotto for weeks on end. I go to the back of the house, where there's a tent pitched for 'rockagers' who now and again want to shake a leg. . . . A busty young girl in jeans slides a disc on the battered gramophone, and some rockagers begin to dance while the Elvis of Presley accuses each and everyone of being 'Nothing but a Hound Dog.'

And some black performers began imitating this new music. "Masihambe," recorded by the Georgetown Boys in early 1957, was described by the music critic of *Zonk* (September 1957) as a "rock 'n' roll Zulu number"; the stage show "Township Rock" at the Johannesburg Town Hall on 7–9 May 1958 featured "Woodpecker's Rock" by the Woody Woodpeckers and "P. J. Rock" by the Jazz Dealers; recorded examples include "Rock by Boogie" by the Bogard Brothers [HMV JP 669] and "Tzaneen Rock" by G. Mabitsela [Drum DR 170].

But within no more than two years after its introduction into black South Africa, rock 'n' roll virtually disappeared. Critics began disparaging it: Blake Modisane shrugged off a new release by the Comets, writing in *Drum* of September 1958: "Come off it, Bill Haley. Nothing's as bad as rock 'n' roll when it's bad. It's nonsense, just too bad to even annoy"; and an anonymous *Drum* critic greeted another rock 'n' roll disc in June 1959 with "Big beat, nonsense lyrics and just a mixture of disorganised sounds. . . doesn't make much of anything. It's good if you don't have to listen to it. Just wiggle to it, friend, because there ain't much more you could do." Record companies, not realizing the profits they had hoped for, pulled back from distributing new rock 'n' roll discs to blacks. And black musicians stopped performing pieces with "rock" in the title. As a result, even though early rock 'n' roll progressed through the stages of importation and imitation—"rock" pieces by black performers were mostly in fast, rhythmic twelve-bar blues form, often with direct melodic borrowing from Bill Haley or Elvis—it never reached the third stage, that of assimilation.

Early rock 'n' roll drew more directly on Afro-American musical styles than had any previous American music available to black South Africans. The recurring harmonic pattern of the twelve-bar blues form is, after all, related to the cyclic patterns of African music. The several instruments (lead guitar, rhythm guitar, saxophone, rhythm) maintain their individuality in some sort of layering. But no elements of early rock 'n' roll penetrated popular African styles. Even the amplified guitar, which gave this music in the United States one of its most characteristic sounds, seems to have reached South Africa through jazz, not rock 'n' roll.[46]

In order to understand this rejection, one must remember that early rock 'n' roll was imported into South Africa by white-controlled record companies for sale to the white youth of the country; distribution among blacks was an afterthought. Only music by white performers was chosen, a decision made by record companies on the grounds that South African whites were unlikely to respond to music by black performers, particularly in the climate of heightened racial tension marking the 1950s. To the best of my knowledge, records by Chuck Berry and Little Richard were not distributed in South Africa at this time. When live "rock" performers were brought to the country, they were all white and mostly British: Tommy Steele, Cliff Richard, Dickie Valentine, Billy Fury, Connie Francis, Dusty Springfield, Pat Boone. Steele scheduled two concerts for black audiences in the Bantu Men's Social Club in Johannesburg during his South African tour of 1958; but the afternoon program took place in an almost empty house, the evening concert drew an audience filling no more than half the hall, and a black observer reported in *The Star* of 3 May 1958 that "Mr. Steele's manners, his comments. . . did not endear him to us."

Though a few musicians recognized rock 'n' roll's stylistic dependency on Afro-American music, the black population as a whole saw it as music by white performers for white audiences, generating controversies among the white population of little concern to blacks. Ironically this music—recognized, praised, and condemned in America as both reflecting and furthering racial integration in the 1950s—was rejected by South African blacks because, from the information available to them, it seemed to be music having to do only with white interests and white power.[47] As before, black African perception of American music and culture had been shaped by the media.

* * *

The twist was another matter.

Hank Ballard & the Midnighters' recording of "The Twist" [King 5171], written by Ballard himself, appeared on *Billboard*'s rhythm-and-blues charts for thirteen weeks in 1960 and also on the "white" charts for sixteen weeks in the summer of that year. But it was a recording of the piece by Philadelphia-born Ernest Evans ("Chubby Checker") for Cameo-Parkway that became an international sensation. Released twice in the United States, in the summer of 1960 and the fall of 1961, it became a #1 hit on the *Billboard* "Hot 100" charts both times and was on the rhythm-and-blues charts for a total of thirteen weeks as well. Within no more than two years of its release, the disc had sold some three million copies.

A typical rhythm-and-blues piece, in twelve-bar blues form with a fast, driving beat, "The Twist" was an anomaly for 1960. By this time the music industry had succeeded in subverting the powerful response to early rock 'n' roll, retaining the term "rock 'n' roll" while substituting a musical style (invoking the aesthetic of latter-day Tin Pan Alley) and a new type of performer (Pat Boone, Paul Anka, Fabian, and a clutch of other "teen idols") more congenial to its own traditions. The success of "The Twist" suggests that the music industry had misjudged public taste by adopting this strategy. But the industry was reflecting—and perhaps helping to shape—a backlash against black gains of the mid-1950s. Southern states were devising ways to resist court-ordered school integration; social integration was proceeding slowly and bitterly; and whites outside of the South, in anticipation of action against racial segregation and discrimination in their areas, were developing their own strategies to maintain the racial status quo.

Chubby Checker's music reached South Africa by way of England, where the two releases of "The Twist" had likewise gone to the top of the charts in both 1960 and 1961. *Zonk* reported in January 1962 that "the Twist, the freshest of the new dances and a vogue in New York entertainment, is the dance that has captivated both young and old in South Africa." A 78-rpm disc pairing Chubby Checker's "The Twist" and "Twistin' USA," released in South Africa in December 1961, was reviewed in *Zonk* (April 1962) as having been "recorded by the king of them all, Chubby Checker, the teenagers' heart-throb. The Americans say nothing has risen so fast outside the Jet Age!" A cover story in the same publication for July, with photographs of twisting black teenagers in Johannesburg and Pietermaritzburg, commented that the dance was either "a depraved, wicked exhibition of sex on the dance floor or a brilliant graceful expression, depending on your point of view."

Within weeks, literally, black South African musicians were recording pieces with "twist" in the title, among them "Zulu Twist" by Victoria Mhlongo and the Durban-ites [Gallo GB 3303], "Hambakahle Twist" by Billy the Kid and Jesse James [Envee NV 3366], "Hamba Njalo Twist" by Sparks Nyembe [Trutone Quality TJ 695], and "New Sound Twist" by Kid Moncho's Hot Beat Kings [Gallo USA 181]. Some of these were more or less literal imitations of the American twist—fast, rhythmic, cast in twelve-bar blues form—but assimilation took place almost immediately. Reggie Msomi's "Get Out Baby Twist" [Gallo USA 206] is instrumental throughout, with five twelve-bar saxophone choruses played by Msomi bracketed by a number of repetitions of an eight-bar phrase built over a repeated harmonic pattern. "Big Five Twist" by Spokes Mashiyane [Gallo New Sound GB 3461], recorded in 1963, is built over the four-chord harmonic cycle I-IV-I-V repeated nineteen times, and the tempo is more moderate than that of the original "The Twist."

By the end of 1963 many hundreds of such Africanized "twist" pieces had been recorded and released in South Africa, and this music and the dance associated with it persisted until 1968–69, much longer than in the United States. Two obvious factors help explain this popularity, so striking in contrast to the fate of rock 'n' roll among black South Africans. First, the twist was associated with black Americans from the beginning. Photographs and journalistic accounts identified Chubby Checker as black, and even though white Americans soon preempted the twist for their own amusement and profit, Africans continued to think of the twist as an Afro-American genre. Chubby Checker thus became the sort of cultural hero and role model in black South Africa that Chuck Berry and Little Richard never had the chance to be. The second factor was that the twist was a dance, with specific though flexible movements associated with the music; this had not been the case with early rock 'n' roll. In order to suggest how congenial this notion is to Africans, I can do no better than quote John Chernoff:

> If you play a recording of American music for an African friend, . . . he may say, as he sits fidgeting in his chair, "What are we supposed to do with this?" He is expressing perhaps the most fundamental aesthetic in Africa: without participation, there is no meaning. When you ask an African friend whether or not he "understands" a certain type of music, he will say "yes" if he knows the dance that goes with it.[48]

The importation, imitation, and assimilation of the twist in South Africa took place against the backdrop of an interlocking series of dramatic and traumatic events.

On 21 March 1960 a confrontation took place in Sharpeville (a black township near Vereeniging) between some five thousand blacks gathered to protest the pass laws,[49] as part of a general campaign organized by the Pan-Africanist Congress (PAC), and three hundred police sent there to control the demonstration. Early in the afternoon,

> a scuffle broke out at the gate which breached the wire fence round the police station. A police officer, accidentally or deliberately, was pushed over. The attention of the front rows was focused on the gate and they surged foward, pushed by people behind them who wanted to see what was happening. At this stage, according to police witnesses, stones were thrown at them. The more inexperienced constables began firing their guns spontaneously. The majority of those killed or wounded were shot in the back. Altogether 69 people died, including eight women and ten children. 180 people were wounded.[50]

Demonstrations, protest meetings, and strikes spreading to Cape Town, Durban, and elsewhere were silenced only when the government declared a state of emergency giving the security forces extraordinary powers of detention, arrest, and civil control. The two chief black nationalist organizations, the PAC and the African National

Congress (ANC), which had followed policies of non-violent protest to this point, were outlawed, and in 1964 many of their leaders, including Nelson Mandela, were sentenced to life imprisonment. Under the leadership of the prime minister, H. F. Verwoerd, the Union of South Africa was reshaped as a republic in 1961, following a referendum of the white voters on the issue of autonomy, and the new Republic of South Africa withdrew from the British Commonwealth to pursue an independent political course. International outrage at the Sharpeville massacre and subsequent events within South Africa brought condemnation and boycotts by the United Nations and many individual countries, forcing the government into the historic Afrikaner position of "laager"—embattled, surrounded by numerically superior hostile forces, determined to battle for survival at all costs. Verwoerd persuaded the vast majority of white South Africans that the country faced a Communist-inspired "total onslaught" from inside and out. His vision of "Separate Development," a much more sophisticated version of racial *apartheid* in which blacks would be citizens of a number of independent "homelands" or "national states" and would be allowed in "white" South Africa only under severely controlled circumstances as a temporary labor force, gradually took shape with the enactment of new legislation, beginning with the Promotion of Bantu Self-Government Act (1959).

The media were intended to play a critical role in maintaining social control over the black population, and in persuading it of the benefits and inevitability of Separate Development. A Bantu Programme Control Board of the SABC, set up in 1960, was charged with the establishment of separate radio services in each of the major African languages of the region, "bringing home to the Bantu population that separate development is, in the first place, self-development through the medium of their own language and that, by this means, there will be progress in all spheres of life."[51] The challenge for the government was to insure that blacks listened to these programs, collectively called Radio Bantu. Recognizing that "[radio] is something which you cannot force on anybody"[52] and that "Music constitutes, and will always constitute, the most comprehensive component of any radio service,"[53] the SABC developed and refined a strategy of using music to draw and hold black listeners to Radio Bantu so that they would also hear news and political commentary, in their own languages, written in Pretoria.

Each "vernacular" service of Radio Bantu had a committee charged with selecting appropriate music; the selection process included screening song lyrics to insure that political and moral sentiments contrary to state policy were not heard on the air. The twist was accepted by strategists and censors as appropriate music for Radio Bantu, since it seemed impossible to read revolutionary content into the song lyrics of Chubby Checker and his peers, and none of them was known to be associated with troublesome political activity. The fact that they sang in English was something of a problem, since one of the aims of Radio Bantu was to stress "tribal" identity—and thus inhibit black unity—through exclusive use of traditional languages, to counter the growing use of English as the common tongue among Africans of different linguistic groups. Since African twist music was instrumental, it was even better suited to Radio Bantu, which accordingly devoted a considerable amount of air time to it.

The government's strategy depended on having a large percentage of the black population listen to Radio Bantu, and its success in achieving this, by helping to make inexpensive transistor radios available and by offering music chosen to appeal to the largest possible audience, was remarkable. Blacks owned 103,000 radio sets in 1962; the number had reached 771,000 by 1966; and two years later (1968) there were more than two million radios in black homes.[54] Thus black radio ownership increased twenty-fold during the lifetime of the African twist; at least some of the proliferation resulted from the popularity of this music. And as elsewhere in the world, radio play stimulated record sales, and in turn recording companies produced more music of the sort already being played on the air. Though the recording industry was in private hands in capitalist South Africa, state policies governing the selection of music for radio play had a considerable impact on record-manufacturing strategy: there was little to be gained from recording music that would not be played on Radio Bantu.

In sum, the early twist was the first genre of Afro-American music to reach black South Africans in essentially the same form in which it was heard by a mass black American audience. In the United States, it was almost immediately co-opted by whites and played little role, symbolic or otherwise, in the continuing struggle for racial equality. In South Africa the twist was more strongly identified with black culture and aspirations, and penetrated deeply into African life. Ironically, in a time of intensified racial repression, the African twist became an effective media weapon in the hands of the racist state.

*   *   *

While it seems impossible to pinpoint just when "soul" was first used as a label for certain types of black American music, and difficult to define its precise musical characteristics, several things can be said with some assurance:

¶ The word was first widely used in 1966–67, in connection with a series of recordings by Percy Sledge ("When a Man Loves a Woman"), Aretha Franklin

("I Never Loved a Man The Way I Love You,"), Wilson Pickett ("Land of 1000 Dances"), and Otis Redding ("I've Been Loving You Too Long" and "Try a Little Tenderness"), among others.

¶ It was adopted as a general label for all black popular music by *Billboard* magazine in 1969.

¶ The style itself was not new in the mid-1960s but had been evolving for many years, particularly in the music of Sam Cooke, Ray Charles, James Brown, and Bobby Bland.

¶ Many soul singers had begun their careers in gospel music, and the characteristically flexible, highly expressive, extravagantly embellished vocal style grew out of black church-music traditions.

¶ Even though white Americans began listening to soul almost immediately, there was little change in musical style as a consequence. Putting it another way, soul was the first Afro-American popular style to enjoy wide dissemination among white audiences without undergoing stylistic transformation at the hands of white arrangers, producers, and entrepreneurs. It was also the first black style resisting imitation by white performers: though some of the latter appropriated elements of soul into their singing, none dared label their music "white soul."

¶ More than any earlier mass-disseminated black style, soul was taken to be an expression of black ethos and black pride.

¶ Soul was contemporary with, and consonant with, a dramatic second push by American blacks to achieve social, educational, and economic equality.

Despite favorable court decisions and the Civil Rights Acts of 1957 and 1960, not even two percent of American blacks were attending integrated schools by the early 1960s, and social integration was proceeding just as slowly. Southern blacks, led by ministers and students, mounted a massive civil disobedience campaign which reached a climax in the summer of 1963. "Blacks filled local jails from Cambridge, Maryland, to Plaquemines Parish, Louisiana, and from Greenville, Mississippi, to St. Augustine, Florida."[55] On 28 August 1963, two hundred thousand people marched, sang, and prayed in Washington in support of more effective civil rights legislation. Black anger directed against continuing racial inequality took more violent form outside the South, with riots in Harlem (1964), Watts (1965), Cleveland (1967), and Detroit (1968), and following the assassination of Martin Luther King, Jr., in 125 cities all over the United States in the spring of 1968.

In order to fight effectively for equality, any oppressed group must first be convinced that it is indeed equal or superior to its oppressors. Much of the history of mass-disseminated "black" music before the 1950s, from minstrel music and "coon" songs of the nineteenth century through such later Tin Pan Alley products as "Shoeshine Boy" (recorded by Louis Armstrong in 1935) and Hoagy Carmichael's "Lazy Bones" and "Rocking Chair" (as recorded by the Mills Brothers), can be read as a continuation of the historic American strategy of depicting blacks as intellectually and morally inferior to whites.[56] Soul music, with its public representation of a positive black image (as epitomized by Aretha Franklin's "Respect" and James Brown's "Say It Loud, I'm Black and I'm Proud"), played an important role in mobilizing and vitalizing black activism in the 1960s and '70s.

Soul, both the music and the concept, reached South Africa quickly. Steve Montjane, writing in the August 1967 issue of *Bona*, reviewed two LP anthologies entitled *Solid Gold Soul* [ALA 9008 and 9018] featuring pieces by Solomon Burke, Wilson Pickett, Joe Tex, Don Covay, Ben E. King, Otis Redding, Percy Sledge, Ray Charles, and Chris Kenner, as well as two LPs by Percy Sledge [ALA 9002 and ALA 9040]. In his column, titled "This Month We Look at 'Soul'," he informed his listeners about "soul jazz":

> Soul Jazz has everything: Blues, pop, rock 'n' roll, lyrics of stirring beauty, philosophy, happiness and dismal sadness, caring and not caring—the lot. Highly sophisticated American techniques, polished English lyrics, but filling us with pride, it is credited with the free, uninhibited emotional content of African music. This is music of Africa which was carried to America during the slave trade and plantations, and is now emancipated to return to Africa still fresh as a breeze, with a heavy rhythm beat—but now sophisticated. Soul Jazz fans will tell you that there is no better music for combining pleasing rhythm with wise instruction and day-to-day problems. Example: Joe Tex, one of the top Soul singers in "Hold What You've Got," says: "Hold what you've got, if you feel you don't want it, throw it away, and you'll see, before you can count 1,2,3, somebody has taken it.". . . He gets to the crux of the problem with sweet music, as is typical of most Soul Jazz numbers.

Three more LPs of "soul jazz" were reviewed in October—"The New Boss" (Joe Tex), "Listen" (Ray Charles), and "I Never Loved a Man" (Aretha Franklin)—and 1968–69 brought the release of still more, by Sam and Dave, Otis Redding, Percy Sledge, Joe Simon, Diana Ross and the Supremes, Brook Benton, and Clarence Carter. *Drum* carried a glossy photo-story on "The King and Queen of Soul" (Percy Sledge and

Aretha Franklin) in its issue of January 1969, further identifying Wilson Pickett as the "Prince" waiting on the sidelines. "Whenever there's a party these days, the records that are most likely to be in danger of wearing out first have the same sound—SOUL," the anonymous writer says, concluding that "Soul is king in South Africa. The music cries out from record players from Muizenburg to Messina!" And it was not only top American soul stars whose music was heard in South Africa: "Soul Cookin'" (1968) by Willie Bobo and other pieces virtually unknown in the United States enjoyed wide distribution in South Africa.

Despite the speed with which soul was imported into South Africa, the second and third phases of penetration were initially problematic. This music was so dependent on the sound of electric instruments (guitars, basses, organs) that imitation and assimilation could not take place without them, and few black Africans had access to the kind of money needed to buy or even rent such equipment. The earliest South African attempts to emulate soul music came from the Cape, with colored (mixed-race) groups. Cape coloreds were sometimes in better economic straits than blacks, and there was also a tradition of racially mixed audiences for musical events in this part of South Africa, making entrepreneurs more willing to subsidize talented non-white musicians. The Fantastics, four colored youths ranging in age from 12 to 14, were able in 1968 to obtain electric instruments costing more than 3,000 rands ($4,500). Their live performances and recordings were "full of electronic drive, short-circuiting the long road to the top in a shower of soul-searing sparks," according to *Drum* (November 1968). The Flames, from Durban, released an LP (*Burning Soul*) which "got a four star billing in America's Billboard magazine," according to *Drum* (April 1968), and the Invaders, from Uitenhagen in the Eastern Cape, "became the first Non-White group to win a golden disc" in South Africa, according to the same source.

By 1969, though, black groups playing "local soul music" had been formed in and around Johannesburg; among the first of these were the Black Hawkes and the Inne Laws. *Bona* (June 1969) carried an account of a musical entertainment for patients and staff at Baragwanath Hospital in Soweto; after an opening of "cool jazz" by the Early Mabuta Quartet,

> Out of the blue came the "Inne Laws"; music that pushed formality and chivelry [*sic*] aside and placed the hall in a frenzy mood. No part of the human joint was not shaking when these boys played "Soul Jazz music." Their music sent the audience sprawling on the ground, some sat shaking on the floor, some lay prostrate on the floor and shook violently, some stood with tears streaming down their cheeks . . . when they played their popular 'Soweto Soul Music'.

This "soul jazz music" of the Inne Laws, the Black Hawkes, and similar early groups—the Soul Giants, the Earthquakes, the Movers, the Teenage Lovers—represented a synthesis of American and African musical elements, rather than mere imitation of American soul. It was purely instrumental, to begin with.[57] The tempo was drastically slower than that of the African twist; the electric organ and solid-body electric guitar were introduced into South Africa with this music; and a few pieces were cast in twelve-bar blues form—all reflections of African familiarity with American soul. But the majority of early African "soul" pieces unfolded over four- or eight-bar harmonic cycles, and melodic lines were repetitious and patterned, reflecting none of the extravagantly embellished vocal lines of American soul.

Black African identification with Afro-American life and culture reached a new peak during this time. Soul reached a larger percentage of the black population than had any earlier styles based on Afro-American music. As the numbers of blacks living in urban areas increased, and the government intensified its campaign to reach the entire black population by means of the mass media, the number of people with access to popular music through radio and phonograph proliferated. American styles of dress, long fashionable among the black elite, became the universal black urban attire, spurred by new strategies of mass production and marketing.

Publications targeted for black readers[58] developed an obsession with black America. *Drum*, a monthly which began publication in 1951, built its circulation on a strategy of "picture features, bright covers, jazz, girls, and crime stories."[59] At least half its stories dealt with black Americans: sports heroes, musicians, flamboyant religious leaders, politicians. American-made goods were advertised, often with pictures of attractive American blacks enjoying the "good life" with the help of these products. But as the 1960s unfolded, *Drum* and similar publications reported increasingly on less positive aspects of black life in America: race riots in urban centers; militant white opposition to the struggle for black voting rights in the South; the assassination of Martin Luther King and the resultant rioting across America; the large number of blacks fighting in Viet Nam; charges of racism brought by black athletes. At the same time, in response to increasing American criticism of apartheid, the SABC and the Afrikaner press intensified their strategy of stressing racial tensions and problems in the United States as a warning against racial mixing in South Africa.[60] Though the government exerted no direct control over independent publications such as *Drum*, it reserved the right to ban publication of information and opinions contrary to its interests and strategies, and the press was wary of questioning state policy. As one of *Drum*'s editors (Tom Hopkinson) said when tendering his resignation, "it was dull work editing a magazine in which almost nothing could be said."[61] As a result of this changing media image of the condition of blacks in America, South African blacks began developing a more complex and realistic view of racial realities in the United States.

Direct contact between South African and American blacks, which had declined anyway during the 1930s and '40s, was a casualty of the early years of Afrikaner rule. It became virtually impossible for an American black to obtain the necessary visa to enter South Africa, or for a black African to have a passport for travel to America. Most black South Africans in the United States were political exiles. Even though South African entrepreneurs had long suspected that a great deal of money was waiting to be made by bringing black American musicians to the country, it was only after twenty years of Afrikaner rule, in 1967, that Abe Hack of Future Promotions received permission from the government for a five-person group headed by singer Laverne Baker to give twenty performances in black townships in and around Johannesburg and Pretoria, including Sharpeville, for black audiences only. There was also a benefit show at Baragwanath Hospital in Soweto.

Even though Baker was little known in South Africa and the peak of her modest career in America had been reached a decade earlier, her shows attracted large and enthusiastic crowds, and her presence in the country piqued the interest of the white press. Judging from published interviews, the government had done an excellent screening job in choosing her as the first black American performer in the country since the Nationalists came to power: she was quoted in *The Star* for 9 June 1967 as saying, "It makes no difference to me what's going on on the political scene," and the same newspaper reported on 14 June that she had no problem with performing before blacks-only audiences, since "I do it at home, in some places where audiences are still segregated." She stayed an extra week in South Africa, expressed interest in coming back and in adopting an African child, and assured reporters that many other black American musicians would welcome the chance to come to the country.

Unlike Baker, Percy Sledge was a top international star when he came to South Africa in 1970. As noted above, he had been labelled "The King of Soul" by the South African press in 1967, and sales of his recordings there topped those of any other black American in the late 1960s and early 1970s. Any remaining doubts about the commercial viability of black American performers in the country, or of the black population's ability and willingness to support them, were swept away by the wildly enthusiastic reception, at times bordering on hysteria, that greeted Sledge's extended series of concerts in black theaters and other township venues across much of South Africa. And it was not only blacks who were eager to hear him perform. The popularity of soul had spread to the white population of South Africa, just as in the United States. At a time when the likes of Patti Page, the Sandpipers, Frankie Laine, and the New

Christy Minstrels made up the imported concert fare for whites-only audiences, the prospect of seeing and hearing a contemporary star of an exciting new genre of popular music excited many whites. But social custom reinforced by the Separation of Social Amenities Act, part of the government's packet of legislation intended to make a reality of Separate Development, prevented whites from attending concerts for black audiences. In a situation almost without precedent in South Africa, blacks had access to something desirable to whites, and the latter were prohibited from sharing it—inspiring many of them to try to crash Sledge's concerts disguised as blacks or Indians.

The South African government, which had been reluctant to allow black American performers in the country, could now see their presence meshing with its own strategies. Blacks performing for blacks in highly publicized events reinforced the image of racial separation; the excitement and pleasure generated among the black population helped divert energy away from more contentious matters. The 1970s brought a stream of black American musicians to South Africa, including Brook Benton, Clarence Carter, Billy Preston, the Commodores, Curtis Mayfield, Millie Jackson, Tina Turner. Entrepreneurs were careful to choose performers with no obvious history of political activity, and to instruct them to avoid controversial statements or contacts while in the country. For its part the government proclaimed these visitors Honorary Whites, allowing them the use of hotels, restaurants, and other facilities normally off-bounds to blacks, very much as Orpheus McAdoo and his troupe had been treated some seventy years before.

Direct contact intensified black South African identification with "soul." Some record producers simply used the label, even for music having nothing to do with the style of American soul. More importantly, however, elements of this music penetrated ever more deeply into indigenous popular styles, synthesizing with more traditional styles at various levels. For instance, "Sala S'thandwa," recorded in 1976 by Izintombi Zesi Manje Manje—a pioneering group in contemporary "vocal jive"—is a traditional Zulu song of farewell, but sung in this recording with harmonies and vocal style obviously indebted to Motown; the disc [GRC 486 MS71] is labeled "Zulu Vocal Soul Jive." But even here, and in the music of similar "soul" groups such as the Movers, the Young People, Cokes and the Midnight Stars, and the Vaal Express, there is little solo singing. As in all vocal jive of the 1960s and '70s, the lead singer interacts with a small vocal group, often in suggestion of traditional call-and-response patterns. It was not until a few years later, after Doby Gray and other American soul singers had performed in South Africa, that Kori Moraba and Babsy Mhlengeni began to emulate the solo vocal style of soul.[62]

In the United States, soul music asserted in practice what the Black Consciousness movement proposed in theory—that black people had a culture as good as, or better than, that of white America, and that this culture should be cultivated with pride. Black Consciousness in South Africa, linked at first with the establishment in 1969 of the all-black South African Students' Organization (SASO), had a somewhat different focus, reflecting the special imperatives of the black situation in that country.

> Its leaders . . . argued that the immediate problem in mobilising black resistance was psychological. Before one could consider the difficulties of organization and strategy the inferiority complexes engendered by oppression and paternalism had to be overcome. Jettisoning any links between black leadership and predominantly white liberal institutions was essential if all traces of a dependency mentality were to be eradicated. White liberals lacked the appropriate motivation to identify fully with black political and social aspirations. More positively, blacks had to create a social identity to replace the concepts generated by white liberal notions of integration into a western capitalist society. To this end blacks should draw on indigenous cultural traditions.[63]

Steve Biko, the most visible leader of South African Black Consciousness, envisaged "a nonracial, just and egalitarian society in which color, creed and race shall form no point of reference,"[64] but he understood that black "group power" was necessary "in the game of power politics."

> Being an historically, politically, socially and economically disinherited and dispossessed group, [blacks] have the strongest foundation from which to operate. The philosophy of Black Consciousness, therefore, expresses group pride and the determination by the Blacks to rise and attain the envisaged self.[65]

American Soul music was accepted by Biko as an expression of black pride growing out of the "indigenous cultural traditions" of black America. But there was a problem with South African "soul jazz" or "soul jive." Its production and dissemination were controlled by white capital, and it was being used with telling effect by the state-run SABC, in its Radio Bantu transmissions, to propagate Separate Development. More generally, the state had preempted the issue of black African "indigenous culture" into its own strategies, attempting to manipulate the several different African languages and cultures to create the impression of greater differences among various "tribal" groups than in fact existed, in order to inhibit black unity. In this world turned upside down, Black Consciousness leaders were faced with a strange dilemma: if they tried to use traditional African culture as a basis for stengthening black social identity and group pride, they risked playing into the government's hands; and they had no access to the mass media to put forward an alternate view. As Muff Andersson has put it, "We can discuss whether a music that stands for the unity of the people should go through any commerical process at all: and to those who believe not, we could argue that some powerful and politically sound music has come through these channels. Unfortunately not too much of this can reach the people it is aimed at, because of the state control of radio and because of controls on other institutions."[66] Thus black radicals of the 1970s, within the country and in exile, largely rejected contemporary commercial, mass-disseminated music in favor of older syncretic genres less contaminated by governmental appropriation—jazz, and the choral "freedom songs" so popular at rallies, funerals, and other mass gatherings.

The irony here is that the "soul jive" rejected by some black political leaders had integrated elements of Afro-American and African styles so successfully that it was instinctively heard and accepted as an expression of black consciousness by its millions of African listeners.

*   *   *

Disco, which dominated American popular music for several years in the mid-1970s, was in some ways more "African" than any other popular genre to date. A typical piece such as Donna Summer's "Love To Love You, Baby" of 1976 used a text of only a few lines, repeated over and over; structurally, most disco pieces were built over a brief, persistently repeating harmonic sequence, underlined by a prominent ostinato-like pattern in the electric bass. Like most African music, disco supplied a continuous, rhythmically insistent sound pattern for dancers, extended over a long enough period of time to carry participants into a state of near-hypnosis.

The roots of disco were in Afro-American music. As far back as the late 1960s Sly Stone was playing fast pieces unfolding over an ostinato-like bass pattern, and the early 1970s brought the sub-genre of "funk"—rhythmic dance music by Edwin Starr, the Ohio Players, and George Clinton underlaid by persistent rhythms and harmonies. Then, as had happened so many times before in American popular music, white performers appropriated a style forged by blacks. K. C. & the Sunshine Band, among other groups, brought out successful pieces of funk; "The Hustle," written and recorded by Van McCoy in 1975, was the archetypical early disco piece; and America's disco culture was formalized in 1977 by the film *Saturday Night Fever* and its soundtrack album, featuring the Bee Gees.

Disco became the most truly interracial popular music since early rock 'n' roll. Performers were both black and white, as were audiences, and other minorities such as Hispanics and gays were identified with this music as well. Its reception also cut across racial, ethnic, and national boundaries; *Saturday Night Fever* not only became the top-selling LP among white Americans in 1977, it was also the first album by white performers (mostly) to reach the top position on *Billboard*'s "Soul LP" chart, while at the same time becoming a best-selling item in Canada, The Netherlands, Portugal, Finland, South Africa, Sweden, Mexico, New Zealand, and France.

For black Americans, the mid-1970s were marked both by highly visible political triumphs—the election of black mayors in several large cities, some high-level black appointments by the Carter administration—and by much slower consolidation of the social and economic gains of the 1960s. Backlash against disco at the end of the decade was an accurate barometer of an increasingly conservative mood in American life, climaxed by the election of Ronald Reagan to the presidency in 1980. Despite media attention focused on white performers, both the music of disco and its cultural milieu were quite correctly understood by most Americans as deriving from minority cultures, particularly Afro-Americans. Mass burning of disco records at baseball games, condemnation of this music by certain disc jockeys, and derogatory songs such as "Disco Sucks" were directed not so much against the music itself as the culture from which it came. For most black Americans, the 1970s reinforced the reality that racial equality was a dream not yet fully realized.

But as had always been the case, black South Africans were confronted with a far more desperate situation than were American blacks. The government's policy of Separate Development had resulted in the forced removal of millions of people to crowded, desolate, remote "homelands."[67] The separate but unequal system of Bantu Education did little more than give a useful level of literacy to the black labor force. No black could vote, at any level; even their township leadership was imposed by the government. The leaders of black unions and other organizations were jailed, banned, or harassed. Student-led protests and demonstrations in the summer of 1976, beginning in Soweto and spreading elsewhere, were met with starkly brutal force, even for South Africa, leaving 575 dead and 2,389 wounded. The Black Consciousness Movement was suppressed, its leaders detained, and Steve Biko died at the hands of security forces, bringing about even more black anger and international outrage. It did not seem a propitious time for a new, totally apolitical genre of popular dance music to flourish in the country, but old patterns persisted: South African record companies released American disco records and the SABC put them on the air; some black performers began recording music imitative of American disco; and elements of this style began penetrating indigenous popular music.

This time, however, there was even less stylistic difference to be mediated than before. Much South African soul jive of the mid-1970s already sounded very much like American disco. "Bump Jive" by the Movers [City Special CYL 1030] unfolds over a persistent harmonic ostinato in a moderate dance tempo, with a prominent electric bass; the LP has only a single piece on each side, each lasting more than fourteen minutes. Though some groups drew on the style of American disco,[68] most South African "disco" music of the late 1970s and early '80s merely appropriated the word as a label for indigenous jive, without a change of style; and the word also began to be used as a general term for dancing in bars and other township locations, to live or recorded music of any type.

Disco music in America has been taken by journalists and social commentators as signaling the beginning of the "me generation" and its narcissist fascination with self at the expense of social consciousness. Disco was in truth a more complex phenomenon than that, both musically and politically. But it was seen abroad, certainly in South Africa, as mindless, apolitical entertainment, and as such it was appropriate music for the government and its agencies to encourage among blacks, in such troubled times. Black South Africans received it as pure entertainment having no connection with the continuing struggle of black Americans for personal and political power and freedom.

*   *   *

Thus the past hundred years has seen a shifting pattern of relations between Afro-American music and culture, and black South Africa.

Until the middle of the present century, virtually all "black" American music imported into South Africa had been doubly mediated: first by entrepreneurs and producers in the United States who shaped it for consumption by white audiences; then by South African entrepreneurs, record companies, and the government for consumption in that country by white consumers. Minstrel songs, spirituals, ragtime, syncopated dance music, and various forms of jazz also became available to South African blacks as urbanization brought more of them into contact with white life and culture, and gave them the economic means to become consumers of Western goods and entertainment. Because of the extremely limited and highly selective nature of the direct contact between American and South African blacks, the latter were in no position to understand that their images of Afro-American music were shaped largely by white media, even when the performers were black, and that they had no access to the genres of black American music now thought to be the "purest" expression of black culture—shouts and spirituals as sung in religious services rather than on the concert stage, rural dance music, field hollers, rural blues, the piano music of black dance halls, New

Orleans jazz, black territorial bands of the 1920s and '30s, early urban blues, gospel music, early rhythm-and-blues. Furthermore, the handful of black South Africans who came to America found themselves unwitting prisoners of black American middle class culture, which at this time was intent on legitimizing itself through emulation of white America.

Throughout the late nineteenth and first half of the twentieth centuries, some black Americans were able to move into more privileged positions (according to standards of American capitalism) than was possible for their brethren in South Africa, and thus Africans were justified in thinking that American blacks had achieved a degree of social and cultural identity and the beginnings of a political power base, in the face of a dominant and often hostile white population. But it is also true that this perception of black American identity and culture was distorted by distance, by the near impossibility of direct contact, and above all by the white-controlled media. To a large extent, the image of the American black which served to focus black African aspirations in the late nineteenth and early twentieth centuries was a false one, or at best grossly incomplete.

As the twentieth century unfolded, black South African perception of Afro-American music and status slowly sharpened. By the 1930s and '40s it was possible for Africans to hear recordings of a considerable body of music performed by black Americans, as opposed to whites parodying black styles. Even though this music was still selected and mediated by whites, blacks in both America and South Africa identified with it because the performers were of their own race, even if the style was still largely white.

The 1950s and '60s brought a major turning point in black American/South African relations, as a result of three factors: a dramatic improvement in the social and political conditions of black Americans; an equally dramatic worsening of most aspects of black life in South Africa under the National Party and its policies of apartheid and Separate Development; and an ever-increasingly realistic African view of black America.

Black South Africans followed the Civil Rights movements in the United States and the rise of Black Consciousness and Black Power. They understood the role that music played in these struggles, in asserting the self-identity and aspirations of black people and in unifying them during mass actions. Soul music was accepted and imitated with even more enthusiasm than earlier genres of Afro-American music, its message of black identity and pride understood and emulated. And Africans realized that, despite some white opposition to political and social integration, the United States was a place where these things *could* happen and were happening, and that both the government and many individual white people were helping to bring them about.

But as the 1970s came and went with virtually no change in black South Africa, the long-cherished dream that the American model of evolutionary, non-violent social and political change could serve for South Africa began to fade. Black Africans tried these strategies time and again, with no results. There could be no *Brown v. Board of Education* in South 'frica, because segregated education was legally institutionalized. There could be no effective Civil Rights movements, because the goals of such action were illegal, not constitutionally protected. Racial inequality was enshrined in South Africa not only in social custom but, more importantly, in law. Black Americans were still admired for their cultural products, but their political condition began to be seen as having little to do with the reality of South Africa. With the 1980s and President Reagan's policy of "constructive engagement," black attitudes toward the United States worsened. Robert Kennedy had been given a hero's welcome in Soweto in the mid-1960s, because he was seen as sympathetic to the black struggle for equality in America and thus represented hope for black South Africa as well. Twenty years later Edward Kennedy was greeted with suspicion and hostility. A frustrated black South Africa, no longer believing that the American Dream represented a solution to its problems, was turning to other models.

Individual black American musicians of the 1980s have enjoyed the same popularity in South Africa as elsewhere in the world. But Michael Jackson, Lionel Richie, and Whitney Houston are taken to be only entertainers, not political and social role models and heroes, and the same is true for local musicians who imitate them—Brenda [Fassie] and the Big Dudes, for example. Black South Africans are now able to hear that this music, heavily mediated by the white-dominated American music industry, is less dynamic and less relevant to their situation than the music of the Soul Brothers, Steve Kekana, and many other contemporary black South African musicians who have managed to create a popular style widely accepted as reflective of the spirit of a new black South Africa, even though the means of production and dissemination have remained in the hands of whites.

In the end, Paul Simon's *Graceland* is symbolic of the beginning of a new era of relations between South Africa and the United States—an era in which the music and culture of black South Africans, and their struggle for freedom, has something important to say to Americans, white and black.

NOTES

[1] Paul Simon, *Graceland* [Warner Brothers 25447; rel. 1986].

[2] For the most comprehensive discussion of this issue, see Robert Christgau, "South African Romance," *Village Voice*, 23 September 1986, pp. 71–73, 84.

[3] Dale Cockrell, "Of Gospel Hymns, Minstrel Shows, and Jubilee Singers: Toward Some Black South African Musics," *American Music* 5/4 (Winter 1987), 417–32.

[4] David B. Coplan, *In Township Tonight! South Africa's Black City Music and Theatre* (Johannesburg: Ravan Press, 1985), p. 38.

[5] Veit Erlmann, "A Feeling of Prejudice: Orpheus M. McAdoo and the Virginia Jubilee Singers in South Africa, 1890–1898," *Journal of Southern African Studies* 14/3 (1987), p. 1–35.

[6] Erlmann's landmark article cited in note 5, gives a detailed account and analysis of this historic episode.

[7] Quoted in Erlmann, "A Feeling of Prejudice," p. 9.

[8] Coplan, *In Township Tonight!*, p. 41

[9] These "Coon Carnivals" in time became great tourist attractions in Cape Town, for whites and blacks alike, and eventually toured in other parts of South Africa and even Europe. They continued until 1986, when the colored community of Cape Town decided not to stage a Carnival, as a protest against increasingly repressive actions by the government.

[10] See Veit Erlmann, "African Popular Music in Durban, 1913–1939" (unpublished), p. 8. For information on black minstrel activity of the 1920s, see Coplan, *In Township Tonight!*, pp. 123–24.

[11] Coplan, *In Township Tonight!*, p. 41.

[12] Erlmann, "African Popular Music," p. 9.

[13] I will avoid use of the term "tribe," which—in addition to being virtually useless ethnographically—has too often been used in a pejorative sense.

[14] The Khoikhoi ("Hottentot") and San ("Bushmen") peoples are exceptions, with their non-Bantu "click" languages; but these languages, like the people who speak them, have virtually disappeared from modern South Africa.

[15] See Monica Wilson and Leonard Thompson (eds.), *A History of South Africa to 1870* (Cape Town & Johannesburg: David Philip, 1985), pp. 75–186, for a discussion of this issue.

[16] Peter Larlham, *Black Theater, Dance, and Ritual in South Africa* (Ann Arbor: UMI Research Press, 1985), particularly pp. 1–59.

[17] Personal communication, 31 May 1984.

[18] For recorded examples of this repertoire, see Veit Erlmann (ed.), *Mbube Roots: Zulu Choral Music from South Africa* [Rounder Records 5025], and V. Erlmann and B. Mthethwa (eds.), *Zulu Songs from South Africa* [Lyrichord LLST 7401].

[19] Cockrell, "Of Gospel Hymns," pp. 2–3, 21.

[20] Erlmann, "African Popular Music," pp. 7, 8, 27.

[21] Yvonne Huskisson, *The Bantu Composers of Southern Africa* (Johannesburg: The South African Broadcasting Corporation, 1969), pp. 96–97.

[22] Wilson and Thompson, *A History of South Africa*, p. 352.

[23] Ibid., pp. 260ff.

[24] For a discussion and interpretation of this episode, see Coplan, *In Township Tonight!*, pp. 41–42.

[25] Coplan, *In Township Tonight!*, p. 43

[26] E. de Waal, "American black residents and visitors in the South African Republic before 1899," *South African Historical Journal* 6 (1974).

[27] George M. Frederickson, *White Supremacy: A Comparative Study in American & South African History* (Oxford: Oxford University Press, 1981), pp. 239–40.

[28] Orpheus McAdoo, writing in the *Southern Workman* of November 1890, as quoted in Erlmann, "A Feeling of Prejudice," p. 5.

[29] From the *Southern Workman* of January 1891, as quoted in Erlmann, "A Feeling of Prejudice," p. 18.

[30] From *Leselinyana* for 1 October 1890, as translated by Naphtalie Morie and quoted in Erlmann, "A Feeling of Prejudice," p. 18.

[31] Charles Hamm, *Music in the New World* (New York & London: W. W. Norton and Company, 1983), pp. 76–82, 183–88, 236–42.

[32] Harry Eskew, "White Urban Hymnody," liner notes for *Brighten the Corner Where You Are: Black and White Urban Hymnody* [New World Records NW 224], pp. 4–6.

[33] Hamm, *Music in the New World*, pp. 133–39, 375–78.

[34] Coplan, *In Township Tonight!*, p. 70 and passim.

[35] David Coplan, "The urbanisation of African music: some theoretical observations," *Popular Music* 2 (1982), pp. 122–23.

[36] Resistance to uncontrolled immigration was first directed at Asians, with the Chinese Exclusion Act of 1882 and the subsequent Japanese and Korean Exclusion Leagues in California. A 42-volume report by a Congressional Committee on Immigration, released in 1910, assembled "scientific" evidence to demonstrate that the new immigrant stock was "racially inferior" to the older population of western and northern Europeans, and a succession of new immigration acts climaxed in 1924 with the exclusion of immigrants from many Asian and African countries and severe limitations on further influx from the Mediterranean area and Central Europe.

[37] Tom Lodge, *Black Politics in South Africa Since 1945* (London and New York: Longman, 1983), p. 1.

[38] For details, see Lodge, *Black Politics*, p. 46.

[39] Lodge, *Black Politics*, p. 71.

[40] This argument is developed in Hamm, *Music in the New World*, pp. 618ff.

[41] Jacques Attali, *Noise: The Political Economy of Music*, trans. Brian Massumi (Minneapolis: University of Minnesota Press, 1985), pp. 11–12, 57–59, and passim.

[42] Hamm, *Music in the New World*, pp. 623–26.

[43] *Sunday Times*, 25 October 1959.

[44] *The Star*, 16 December 1956.

[45] *Annual Report of the South African Broadcasting Corporation* (Pretoria, 1966), p. 6.

[46] Enoch Tabete, perhaps inspired by Charlie Christian, was using an amplified guitar for jazz in the late 1940s and early 1950s. "Thula" [HMV JP 129] is an excellent recorded example of his playing.

[47] For more on this matter see Charles Hamm, "Rock 'n' roll in a very strange society," *Popular Music* 5 (1985), 159–74.

[48] John Miller Chernoff, *African Rhythm and African Sensibility* (Chicago: University of Chicago Press, 1979), p. 23.

[49] The Native Labour Regulation Act of 1911 had required black males to carry identity passes at all times; a revised act of 1952 made it mandatory for all blacks over the age of sixteen, male and female, to have such passes in their possession at all times. Failure to present this "dompas" on demand resulted in immediate arrest and imprisonment. An estimated half-million blacks were arrested each year for violations of the pass laws.

[50] Lodge, *Black Politics*, p. 210.

[51] *Annual Report of the South African Broadcasting Corporation* (Pretoria, 1967), p. 10.

[52] *Debates, The Senate of the Union of South Africa*, Third Session, 12th Parliament, 1960, pp. 2446–47.

[53] *Annual Report of the South African Broadcasting Corporation* (Pretoria, 1964) p. 8.

[54] These figures are from the annual reports of the SABC for these years.

[55] Stephan Thernstrom (ed.), *Harvard Encyclopedia of American Ethnic Groups* (Cambridge and London: The Belknap Press of Harvard University Press, 1980), p. 20.

[56] Further on this point, see Roger Hewitt, "Black through white: Hoagy Carmichael and the cultural reproduction of racism," *Popular Music* 3 (1983), pp. 33–52.

[57] One of the rare exceptions, "The Way That You Love Me," recorded by The Anchors in 1969 [City Special CYB 47], is much more in the Motown style of Diana Ross and the Supremes than an imitation of Aretha Franklin or other soul singers.

[58] Though there was a tradition of African-language publications edited by blacks early in the century, the policies of the National Party brought about a political and economic climate in the 1950s in which "no African newspaper in South Africa was owned or controlled by Africans." (F. Barton, *The Press of Africa: Persecution and Perseverance* [New York, 1979], p. 196.)

[59] Anthony Sampson, *DRUM: An African Adventure—and Afterwards* (London: Hodder and Stoughton, 1983), p. 33.

[60] According to the annual report of the SABC for 1967, among the "talks" broadcast that year on the subject of racial mixing in America were "A sordid chapter in American degradation" (February), "The riot season in the United States" (June), "Flaming cities illustrate a fallacy" (July), "Negro riots open eyes" (August), and "Integration fosters hate" (November).

[61] Sampson, *DRUM*, p. 293.

[62] Examples of solo singers emulating American soul singers include *The Minerals and Kori Moraba* [RPM 7040, 1978] and *Zulu Soul Vocal* [Gallo, Mavuthela Music, Ziya Duma TL 519, 1978].

[63] Lodge, *Black Politics*, p. 323.

[64] Steve Biko and Millard Arnold (ed.), *Black Consciousness in South Africa* (New York: Vintage Books, 1979), p.v.

[65] Ibid., p. xx.

[66] Muff Andersson, *Music in the Mix: The Story of South African Popular Music* (Johannesburg: Ravan Press, 1981), p. 178.

[67] See Laurine Platzky and Cherryl Walker, *The Surplus People: Forced Removals in South Africa* (Johannesburg: Ravan Press, 1985), and Joseph Lelyveld, *Move Your Shadow: South Africa, Black and White* (New York: Penguin Books, 1986), pp. 119–54, for accounts of the ruthless "social engineering" involved in forcing blacks to live in the so-called homelands.

[68] The Johannesburg-based black band Harari had considerable success with American-style disco music in the late 1970s and early 1980s. See "Get Up and Dance" on *Flying Out* [Gallo MC 4537, 1981) and "Boogie Through the Night" on *Street Sounds* [Gallo HUC 501, 1983].

Charles Hamm, Arthur R. Virgin Professor of Music at Dartmouth College, is a distinguished musicologist and past president of the American Musicological Society. He is noted especially for the breadth of his scholarly interests—from music of the Renaissance to that of today, from the most artful art music to pop and rock, from American to South African music. His major works in American music have been the books *Yesterdays: Popular Song in America* (1979) and *Music in the New World* (1983), a comprehensive history of United States music. He is now completing a book on his latest interest: *All That Jive: South African Popular Music in the Rock Era.* The present monograph, reflecting that interest, is a revision of two public lectures Professor Hamm delivered during his tenure as I.S.A.M. Senior Research Fellow in 1986–87.

The Institute for Studies in American Music at Brooklyn College, City University of New York, is a division of the College's Conservatory of Music. It was established in 1971. The Institute contributes to American-music studies in several ways. It publishes a series of monographs, a periodical newsletter, and special publications of various kinds. It serves as an information center and sponsors conferences and symposia dealing with all areas of American music including art music, popular music, and the music of oral tradition. The Institute also encourages and supports research by offering fellowships to distinguished scholars and, for assistance in funded projects, to junior scholars as well. The Institute supervises the series of music editions *Recent Researches in American Music* (published by A–R Editions, Inc.) and is the administrative seat of the Charles Ives Society. I.S.A.M. activities also include presentation of concerts and lectures at Brooklyn College for students, faculty, and the public.